I0504541

TABLE OF CONTENTS

Introduction

About Me, Esad Kılıç

Hello, I'm Esad Kılıç. Ever since I was little, I've always been fascinated by the sheer transformative power of technology. From a young age, I was curious about how things worked and how I could make them better.

My journey as an entrepreneur and finance enthusiast has been shaped by diverse experiences across different industries and countries. From my early ventures in HR to my current role as the Co-Founder of ARspar Technologies, I have constantly sought opportunities to make an impact and drive innovation.

One of my initial professional experiences was working as an SME Advisor at a bank. This role allowed me to delve into the intricacies of financial management and gain a deeper understanding of the challenges faced by small and medium-sized enterprises. It was during this time that my passion for entrepreneurship began to flourish.

Driven by an entrepreneurial spirit, I embarked on several ventures that pushed me to think outside the box and embrace innovative approaches. My journey took me to different corners of the globe, immersing me in diverse cultures and industries.

As my journey continued, I embraced a new challenge as a Business Development Manager for a health supplier in Belgium. This role allowed me to explore the intersection of finance and healthcare, further expanding my knowledge and expertise.

Currently, I primarily am focused on ARspar Technologies which I co-founded and scaled to 6 figured in the span of a few years while building a team of around 20 people around it. In the company, I am focused on the financial aspects and strategic direction of the business. Our mission is to change the product visualisation space by using the power of Artificial Intelligence, 3D modeling, and Augmented Reality.

My experiences have instilled in me a deep appreciation for entrepreneurship, finance, and the power of innovation. This book is a culmination of my journey, as well as the knowledge and insights I have gained along the way. I am excited to share with you the strategies, best practices, and lessons I have learned in building and scaling successful SaaS businesses.

Join me as we dive into the world of SaaS entrepreneurship and unlock the secrets to building a profitable software service company. Together, we will navigate the challenges, embrace innovation, and unleash the potential for success in this dynamic industry.

My Journey in the SaaS Industry

My journey into the SaaS industry has been one of constant learning and adaptation. As I led the growth of our product visualisation software, I navigated complex software development cycles, customer retention challenges, and everything else that comes with running a SaaS company. It was a challenging yet exciting journey that tested and ultimately strengthened my entrepreneurial skills.

Moreover, I have advised various companies all around Europe for their growth strategies and the foundation for their SaaS business.

The SaaS Industry Through My Eyes

The SaaS industry is a vibrant, ever-evolving landscape that thrives on innovation and convenience. Thanks to the advent of cloud technology, businesses today consume software services in a way that's far more scalable and affordable than ever before. As a part of this industry, I've experienced first-hand how SaaS companies deliver applications over the internet, negating the need for businesses to install and maintain software or manage infrastructure while also allowing the entrepreneur to build a profitable business around the provision of this service.

Why I Wrote This Book

I wrote "SaaS Unlocked: Your Comprehensive Guide to Building a Profitable Software Service" as a practical guide for you, whether you're an aspiring entrepreneur, a startup founder, or a business leader looking to make your mark in the SaaS world.

In the coming chapters, I will share my experiences and insights about formulating a winning SaaS idea, building a robust product, navigating the legal and intellectual property aspects, devising effective pricing strategies, and mastering sales and marketing tactics. Moreover, I will guide you on how to ensure customer satisfaction, scale your company, secure funding for your venture, and maintain its growth sustainably.

My hope is that, by sharing my own journey, lessons, and strategies, I can provide you with a comprehensive roadmap to SaaS success. Whether you're just starting or looking to grow your existing SaaS business, this book will equip you with the knowledge and tools to navigate and thrive in this dynamic industry. So, let's embark on this journey together.

Chapter 1: Understanding the SaaS Model

As we dive into the core of this book, it's crucial to lay a solid foundation by thoroughly understanding what Software as a Service (SaaS) is all about. Over the years, I've come to appreciate that a deep comprehension of the SaaS model forms the basis for all subsequent steps in creating, launching, and scaling a successful SaaS company.

What is SaaS?

In the simplest terms, SaaS is a software distribution model where a service provider hosts applications for customers and makes them available over the internet. This is a departure from traditional models where companies would have to install and run software applications on their own computers or servers. The SaaS model, therefore, eliminates the need for physical software distribution, making it a cost-effective and convenient option for businesses. Some relevant examples of SaaS companies that you probably are also familiar with are: Adobe Creative Cloud, Hubspot, and Slack.

But there's so much more to SaaS than convenience. The beauty of the SaaS model lies in its ability to provide customers with continual software updates, scalability based on business needs, flexible payments, and global accessibility. All you need is an internet connection, and you can access your services from anywhere, anytime.

The Advantages of SaaS

One of the reasons I've been so drawn to the SaaS industry is the plethora of advantages it offers to both businesses and end users. Here are a few:

- Reduced time to benefit: Traditional software requires installation, configuration, and in some cases, additional hardware. All these can significantly delay the time before a user can actually benefit from the software. SaaS applications, on the other hand, are usually ready-to-use as soon as they're purchased.

- Lower costs: SaaS has a differential pricing model which typically involves a monthly or annual subscription fee. This approach can be more cost-effective than the high upfront costs and ongoing maintenance fees associated with traditional software.

- Scalability and integration: As your business grows, you can easily scale your SaaS applications according to your needs. Also, most SaaS vendors offer integration with other SaaS applications, further increasing their versatility and efficiency.

- New releases (upgrades): With SaaS, the service provider manages all updates and upgrades, eliminating the need for users to download or install software patches. You always have access to the latest versions.

- Easy to use and perform proof of concepts: SaaS offerings are easy to use since they already come with best practices and samples inside it. Users can do proof of concepts and test the software functionality or a new release feature at no additional cost.

The SaaS Market & Trends

The SaaS market is a rapidly growing sector of the tech industry. According to a report by Gartner, the global SaaS market is projected to reach over $140 billion by the end of 2023. As the market grows, it's essential for you as a SaaS entrepreneur to keep an eye on emerging trends.

Understanding these trends will help you anticipate changes in the industry, adapt your business accordingly, and gain a competitive advantage. For example, we're seeing an increased emphasis on mobile compatibility and user-centric design in SaaS products, reflecting changes in the way users interact with software.

We're also witnessing the emergence of AI and machine learning in the SaaS world. These technologies allow businesses to offer more personalized, efficient, and intuitive services.

Whether it's keeping track of new technologies, adjusting to shifts in customer behavior, or navigating through the global economic landscape, staying updated with the latest SaaS trends is vital for the growth and sustainability of your SaaS business.

As we continue this journey, remember that understanding SaaS is not a one-time event but a continual process. The world of SaaS is dynamic, and as we delve deeper into subsequent chapters, we'll keep revisiting and expanding on these concepts to provide you with a comprehensive picture of what it takes to succeed in this industry.

Chapter 2: Formulating Your SaaS Idea

Creating a successful SaaS company starts with an idea - a solution to a problem that your potential customers are facing. In this chapter, I'll share some strategies I've used in my own journey to generate and validate SaaS ideas, and introduce you to some tools and resources that can help you do the same.

Identifying Opportunities in the Market

The first step in formulating your SaaS idea is to identify opportunities in the market. These opportunities often lie in gaps in existing products or services, emerging trends, or unsolved problems in a specific industry.

Start by immersing yourself in the industry you're interested in. Join online forums, subscribe to industry newsletters, attend webinars and conferences, and engage with thought leaders on social media. Some resources I found invaluable in my own journey are:

- Gartner: An excellent source for tech trends and market research.
- Product Hunt: A great platform to see what's new and trending in the tech world.
- Reddit: There are numerous subreddits such as r/SaaS, r/startups, and r/Entrepreneur where you can connect with like-minded individuals and discuss the latest industry developments

  .

Understanding Customer Needs

Once you've identified an opportunity, it's essential to understand the needs of your potential customers. Conduct surveys, interviews, or focus group discussions to gain insights into their challenges and desires. Here are a two tools that can help:

- SurveyMonkey: A versatile tool for creating online surveys.
- Typeform: Another excellent tool for engaging and interactive surveys.

Unique Selling Proposition (USP)

Your USP is what differentiates your SaaS product from others in the market. It's the reason why customers would choose your product over your competitors'. Once you've identified an opportunity and understood your customers' needs, think about what unique value you can bring to the table.

For instance, can your product do something that no other product can? Does it solve a problem in a unique way? Does it cater to a specific niche that other products have overlooked? A clear and compelling USP can make your product stand out in a crowded market.

Validating Your SaaS Idea

Before you proceed with building your product, it's crucial to validate your idea. This will save you from investing time and resources into a product that the market doesn't need or isn't willing to pay for.

- Landing Page: Create a simple landing page describing your product's value proposition and see if people are interested enough to sign up for more information. Tools like Unbounce or Instapage can help you set up a professional-looking landing page quickly.
- Crowdfunding: Platforms like Kickstarter or Indiegogo allow you to gauge public interest in your product and also raise funds.
- Beta Program: Launch a beta version of your product to a limited audience. This allows you to test the viability of the product, gather feedback, and make necessary improvements before a full-scale launch. BetaList is a platform where you can launch your beta product to early adopters.

In the coming chapters, we'll dive deeper into how to create a robust SaaS product, covering aspects such as building a dedicated team, deciding on the right technology stack, and more.

Chapter 3: Building Your Saas Product

After validating your SaaS idea, the next critical step is to start building your product. This chapter will guide you through the necessary steps, from assembling a talented team to choosing the right technology stack, developing your Minimum Viable Product (MVP), and adhering to the best security practices.

Assembling Your Team

Building a successful SaaS product is a team effort. You'll need skilled individuals who are not only proficient in their respective fields but also share your vision for the product. Here's a basic outline of the key roles you'll need to fill:

- Product Manager: They will guide the strategy, roadmap, and feature definition for the product.
- Software Developers: A team of developers will handle the actual coding of your SaaS product.
- UI/UX Designers: They will ensure your product is user-friendly and visually appealing.

- Quality Assurance (QA) Specialists: They will test your product to make sure it's bug-free and working as expected.

- Sales and Marketing Team: This team will be responsible for bringing your product to the market and attracting customers.

Note that you do not need a full team before starting out, this is the general guidelines for what you can scale to over time. Platforms like LinkedIn, AngelList, and Glassdoor can be great resources for recruiting your team.

Choosing the Right Technology Stack

The technology stack you choose will have a significant impact on your product's performance, scalability, and future maintenance. While the choice largely depends on your product's specific requirements and your team's expertise, here are some popular choices among SaaS businesses:

- Front-end Development: JavaScript (with libraries and frameworks such as React, Angular, or Vue.js) is widely used for developing interactive user interfaces.

- Back-end Development: Node.js, Ruby on Rails, Django (Python), and Laravel (PHP) are some common choices for server-side development.
- Database Management: PostgreSQL, MySQL, and MongoDB are widely adopted for handling data.
- Cloud Services: Amazon Web Services (AWS), Google Cloud, and Microsoft Azure offer a range of services for hosting, storage, and more.

Remember, there's no one-size-fits-all tech stack for SaaS. Your choice should be based on your specific needs and your team's proficiency.

Building Your Minimum Viable Product (MVP)

An MVP is a version of your product with just enough features to satisfy early customers and provide feedback for future product development. It allows you to test your product in the market without investing too many resources upfront.

Several tools can aid in the process of building your MVP, including:

- Trello or Jira: For project management and tracking progress.
- GitHub: For version control and source code management.
- Slack: For team communication.

Security Practices

With the increasing number of cyber threats, ensuring the security of your SaaS product is crucial. Here are a few best practices:

- Implement SSL: Secure Sockets Layer (SSL) encrypts data between your users' web browser and your server, protecting it from being intercepted.
- Regularly Update and Patch Your Software: Keeping your software up-to-date ensures you're protected from known vulnerabilities.
- Use a Web Application Firewall (WAF): A WAF can protect your application from common exploits and vulnerabilities.
- Data Backup: Regularly back up your data to prevent data loss in case of a cyberattack.

Companies like Cloudflare provide a range of services, including SSL, WAF, and DDoS protection, that can help secure your SaaS product.

Building your SaaS product is an exciting phase in your journey. In the next chapter, we will delve into the legal considerations to keep in mind as you bring your SaaS company to life.

Chapter 4: Legal Considerations for Your SaaS Company

Launching your SaaS company involves not only tech and business decisions but also legal considerations. Understanding these legal aspects is crucial to protect your company from potential legal disputes and liabilities. In this chapter, we will explore some of the key legal elements you should be aware of when setting up your SaaS company.

Establishing a Legal Entity

Your first step should be to establish a legal entity for your business. This entity separates your personal assets from your company's liabilities, providing a critical layer of personal protection. Here are a few options:

- Sole Proprietorship: This is the simplest business structure where the individual entrepreneur owns the business.
- Partnership: If you're starting the business with one or more partners, a partnership could be an option.
- Limited Liability Company (LLC) or Corporation: These structures provide personal liability protection, which separates your personal assets from your business liabilities.

For a SaaS company, forming an LLC or a Corporation is generally advisable due to the liability protection and ease of raising capital. However, each business structure has its own pros and cons. Consulting with a business attorney or a business formation service like LegalZoom or Rocket Lawyer can help you make the right choice.

Intellectual Property (IP) Protection

Your software, logo, domain name, and even your product's name are all intellectual properties. Protecting these is essential to prevent others from using them without your consent.

- Trademark: You can trademark your product's name, logo, and tagline to protect them from being used by others in your industry. If you live in the United States, you can use the United States Patent and Trademark Office's (USPTO) online system to register a trademark.

- Copyright: As soon as you create your software, it's automatically protected by copyright law. However, registering your copyright can provide stronger protection.

- Patent: If your software includes a unique process or method, you might consider obtaining a patent. Consult with a patent attorney or use an online service like LegalZoom.

Privacy Policy and Terms of Service

Having a comprehensive Privacy Policy and Terms of Service is mandatory for a SaaS business.

- Privacy Policy: This document details how you collect, use, and manage your users' personal data. Tools like Termly can help you generate a custom Privacy Policy.

- Terms of Service: This agreement outlines the rules and guidelines for using your service. It can protect you from potential liabilities and disputes.

Data Security Laws and Regulations

Depending on where your customers are located, different data security laws and regulations might apply to your SaaS company. For example, if you have customers in the European Union, you'll need to comply with the General Data Protection Regulation (GDPR). In the United States, different states have different data privacy laws. Consulting with a legal expert who's familiar with SaaS businesses can help you navigate these legal requirements and ensure your business is compliant. In the next chapter, we'll switch gears and delve into the strategies for effectively marketing your SaaS product.

Chapter 5: Marketing Your Saas Product

Now that you have your SaaS product developed and legally secured, it's time to broadcast it to the world. This chapter will walk you through some vital marketing strategies that can help you attract, engage, and retain customers. In the competitive landscape of SaaS, marketing can be the differentiator between your product and your competitors'.

Building a Strong Online Presence

Your online presence serves as the storefront of your SaaS business. It helps potential customers find your product, learn more about it, and ultimately, decide to subscribe.

Website: This is your primary touchpoint with potential customers. It should be professionally designed and easy to navigate. Clearly articulate your product's value proposition, features, pricing, and the problem it solves. Include customer testimonials and case studies to build trust. Tools like Squarespace, WordPress, and Wix offer templates and customizable options to help you build an attractive, user-friendly website.

SEO (Search Engine Optimization): SEO is the practice of optimizing your website so that it ranks higher on search engine results pages (SERPs). Use keyword research tools like Google Keyword Planner or SEMrush to identify relevant keywords in your industry. Incorporate these keywords into your website's content, meta tags, and URLs. Ensure your site is mobile-friendly and has a fast load time to improve your SEO ranking.

Content Marketing: This is a powerful way to attract organic traffic, educate your audience about your product, and establish your brand as an industry thought-leader. Develop high-quality blog posts, ebooks, white papers, webinars, and infographics that provide value to your audience. Content marketing platforms like Medium, LinkedIn, and your own website blog can be effective for publishing and sharing your content.

Social Media: Your target customers are likely to be active on social media platforms. Identify the platforms they frequent and maintain an active presence there. Regularly share valuable content, interact with your audience, and respond to queries or comments promptly. Use tools like Hootsuite or Buffer to schedule posts and manage your social media profiles across multiple platforms.

Paid Advertising

Investing in paid advertising can give your product visibility among a larger audience, generate leads, and drive traffic to your website.

Search Engine Advertising: Google AdWords allows you to run ads that appear on Google search results pages. These ads are displayed when users search for keywords that you bid for, enabling you to reach users who are actively looking for solutions that your product provides.

Social Media Advertising: Platforms like Facebook and LinkedIn offer targeted advertising options that allow you to reach users based on their demographics, interests, and behaviors.

Email Marketing

Email marketing is a highly effective strategy for nurturing leads and engaging existing customers.

- Lead Nurturing: When potential customers sign up for your mailing list or download a resource from your site, they become leads. You can nurture these leads by regularly sending them valuable content, product updates, and personalized offers.
- Customer Retention: For existing customers, send regular newsletters, feature updates, and exclusive offers to keep

them engaged and remind them of the value your product offers.

Mailchimp or ConvertKit are robust tools for managing your email campaigns, automating personalized messages, and tracking performance.

Influencer and Affiliate Marketing

Partnering with influencers and affiliates can expose your product to their audience and bring in more potential customers.

- Influencer Marketing: Identify influencers in your industry who have a large following and a voice that resonates with your target customers. They can promote your product through social media posts, blog posts, or webinars.

- Affiliate Marketing: Affiliates promote your product to their audience and earn a commission for each new customer they bring in. This can be an effective way to reach new customers while only paying for results.

Product Launch

When your product is ready for the market, a strategic launch can generate buzz and drive initial sign-ups.

Launch Event: Host a live event (in-person or online) to introduce your product. Use this opportunity to demonstrate your product's features, share your vision, and answer any questions.

Press Release: Send out a press release to relevant media outlets and industry bloggers to spread the word about your launch.

Social Media and Email Campaign: Promote your launch extensively on social media and through email newsletters to create anticipation among your audience.

Launch on Product Hunt: This platform is popular for discovering new tech products. A successful launch on Product Hunt can bring significant visibility and initial users for your product.

Continuous Customer Feedback

Keep the lines of communication open with your customers even after the launch. Regularly request and act on their feedback to improve your product and meet their evolving needs.

In the next chapter, we'll discuss customer support and service, a crucial aspect for the success and growth of your SaaS business.

Chapter 6: Fundraising, Investors, and Growing Your SaaS Company

Every SaaS startup reaches a point where they need to consider scaling their operations, and this usually requires substantial financial resources. For this reason, fundraising often becomes a crucial step in the growth journey of a SaaS company. In this chapter, we'll delve deep into the intricacies of fundraising, interacting with investors, and ultimately using these resources to fuel the growth of your SaaS business.

Understanding Different Funding Stages

First, it's important to understand the different stages of startup funding:

Pre-Seed Funding: This is the earliest stage of funding, often coming from the founders, friends, or family. Funds at this stage are usually used to develop a prototype or MVP (Minimum Viable Product).

Seed Funding: This is the first official equity funding stage. It typically involves the business owner pitching their idea to micro venture capitalists and angel investors. Seed funding is primarily used to finance the initial stages of market research and product development.

Series A, B, C Funding, and so on: As the startup grows, it goes through several rounds of funding. Each round serves to finance different stages of the business - from user base expansion, product development, to scaling operations and beyond.

Fundraising Strategy

Crafting a fundraising strategy requires careful planning and a thorough understanding of your business model, valuation, and growth prospects.

Understanding Your Needs: First, determine how much funding you need and how you plan to use it. Are you aiming to grow your team, invest in new technology, boost marketing efforts, or expand to new markets?

Valuation: You'll need to establish a valuation for your company. This is often a challenging task for early-stage startups since it's based on future potential rather than existing assets. A financial advisor can help you come up with a reasonable valuation based on your current traction, revenue, market size, and the competitive landscape.

Pitch Deck: Create a compelling pitch deck to present to potential investors. This should clearly articulate your business idea, market size, business model, competitive advantage, team, and financial projections.

Approaching Investors

Once you have your fundraising strategy in place, it's time to approach potential investors. This can be a nerve-wracking process, but being well-prepared can increase your chances of success.

Research: Not all investors are the same. Some specialize in certain industries or stages of business. Conduct thorough research to identify investors who might be interested in your product and are aligned with your vision.

Networking: Leverage your personal and professional network to get introductions to potential investors. Attend industry events, conferences, and meetups. Platforms like LinkedIn and AngelList can also be helpful for connecting with investors.

Pitching: During the pitch meeting, present your idea confidently and be prepared to answer tough questions about your business. Remember, investors are not just investing in a business, they're investing in a team. Show them why you and your team are capable of turning your vision into reality.

Follow-up: After the pitch meeting, send a thank-you note and keep the investor updated on your progress. This keeps the line of communication open and shows your professionalism.

Negotiating and Closing the Deal
Once an investor shows interest in your startup, you'll move into the negotiation stage. This often involves discussions around valuation, investment amount, and terms of the deal. It's recommended to have

a lawyer present during this process to ensure that your interests are protected.

After both parties agree on the terms, you'll sign a term sheet and eventually close the deal. Remember, accepting an investment is not just about getting funding. It's about starting a partnership that will have a significant impact on your business. Choose your investors wisely.

Using the Funds to Grow Your Business

Once you've secured the funding, it's time to put those funds to work. Based on your business plan and the areas you've identified for growth, you can allocate the funds accordingly. Whether it's for hiring more talent, investing in R&D, increasing marketing efforts, or expanding to new markets, make sure every dollar is spent in a way that brings you closer to achieving your business goals.

Fundraising can be a complex and challenging process, but when done right, it can fuel the growth and success of your SaaS business. In the next chapter, we'll discuss customer support and service - another essential element in building a successful SaaS business.

Chapter 7: Customer Support and Service for Your SaaS Business

In a SaaS business model, customer support and service play a crucial role in driving customer satisfaction, retention, and ultimately, recurring revenue. In this chapter, we'll delve into strategies to create a robust customer support system and foster long-term relationships with your users.

Understanding the Importance of Customer Support in SaaS

The subscription-based nature of SaaS businesses necessitates ongoing customer interactions. Unlike traditional one-time purchase software, SaaS customers make recurring payments, and their decision to continue their subscription heavily relies on the quality of service and support they receive.

Furthermore, excellent customer service can lead to upselling and cross-selling opportunities, foster customer loyalty, and generate positive word-of-mouth, all of which contribute to the growth and success of your SaaS business.

Establishing a Robust Customer Support System

Helpdesk Software: Invest in a reliable helpdesk software that helps manage and streamline customer support requests. Platforms like Zendesk, Freshdesk, or Intercom can be invaluable for managing tickets, automating responses, and tracking customer interactions.

Multi-Channel Support: Offer support through multiple channels—email, live chat, phone, social media, etc. This ensures that customers can reach out through their preferred method and receive timely assistance.

Knowledge Base: Develop a comprehensive knowledge base or FAQ section on your website. It should cover common questions or issues users might face, which can help reduce the load on your customer support team.

Self-Service Options: Today's customers appreciate the ability to solve their problems independently. Offering self-service options, like in-app guides, how-to videos, and chatbots can enhance the user experience.

Delivering Exceptional Customer Service

User Onboarding: Your relationship with a customer starts from the moment they sign up. An effective onboarding process helps new users understand how to get the most out of your product. Tools like Appcues or Userpilot can help you create interactive in-app onboarding experiences.

Proactive Support: Don't wait for users to reach out with problems. Monitor usage data to identify common challenges and address them proactively through in-app messages, emails, or webinars.

Personalized Service: Personalize your communication based on user behavior and preferences. This shows customers that you understand their needs and are committed to helping them succeed.

Regular Check-ins: Regularly check in with customers to understand their needs and gather feedback. This not only helps improve your product but also builds stronger relationships with customers.

Building a Customer-Centric Culture

Your entire team—not just the support team—should understand the value of customer-centricity. Encourage all team members to think from the customer's perspective and align their work towards enhancing customer satisfaction. Regular training, sharing customer feedback, and recognizing employees who deliver exceptional customer service can help in fostering a customer-centric culture.

In the next chapter, we'll look at strategies to measure and improve the performance of your SaaS business. Monitoring key metrics and continually optimizing your strategies are crucial to achieving sustainable growth and success.

Chapter 8: Measuring and Improving the Performance of Your SaaS Business

SaaS companies operate in a dynamic and competitive environment where customer preferences and market trends can change rapidly. Hence, it's crucial to measure the performance of your business and constantly look for improvement opportunities. In this chapter, we'll delve into key performance indicators (KPIs) and strategies for performance improvement.

Understanding Key SaaS Metrics

To measure the success and health of your SaaS business, you need to monitor several specific metrics:

Monthly Recurring Revenue (MRR): This is the amount of revenue your business can reliably expect every month. MRR is crucial for understanding your revenue growth and for planning future business decisions.

Annual Recurring Revenue (ARR): This metric is similar to MRR but calculated on a yearly basis. It's an important measure of your company's growth trajectory.

Customer Acquisition Cost (CAC): This is the total cost of acquiring a new customer, including marketing and sales expenses. Keeping CAC low while increasing customer lifetime value (CLV) is crucial for the sustainability of your business.

Customer Lifetime Value (CLV): This measures the total revenue you can expect from a customer over their lifespan with your business. The higher the CLV compared to CAC, the more profitable your business will be.

Churn Rate: This is the rate at which customers stop subscribing to your service. A high churn rate can be a sign of customer dissatisfaction and can seriously impact your MRR.

Net Promoter Score (NPS): This measures customer satisfaction and loyalty. An NPS survey asks customers how likely they are to recommend your service to others.

Tools like Baremetrics, ChartMogul, and Sisense can help you track these metrics.

Improving Your SaaS Performance

Once you understand your current performance, the next step is to take actions to improve. Here are a few strategies:

Optimize Your Pricing Strategy: Pricing can significantly impact your revenue and customer acquisition. Make sure your pricing model aligns with the value your customers receive. Regularly review and adjust your pricing strategy as needed.

Improve Your Onboarding Process: A smooth onboarding process can reduce churn and improve customer satisfaction. Consider using in-app walkthroughs, personalized training, and responsive support during the onboarding phase.

Enhance Customer Support: As discussed in the previous chapter, excellent customer support can increase customer loyalty and reduce churn. Continually look for ways to improve your customer support.

Invest in Product Development: Listen to your customers' feedback and invest in improving your product based on their needs and expectations.

Implement Upselling and Cross-Selling: Encourage existing customers to purchase premium plans or other services you offer. This can increase your MRR and CLV.

Regularly Review and Update Your Sales and Marketing Strategy: The effectiveness of sales and marketing strategies can change over time. Regularly review your strategies and make necessary adjustments based on their performance.

Remember, the key to improving performance is a combination of regular monitoring, quick learning, and continuous implementation of changes. In the next chapter, we'll explore strategies to ensure the sustainability and long-term success of your SaaS business.

Chapter 9: Ensuring the Sustainability and Long-Term Success of Your SaaS Business

Building a SaaS business is a complex and continuous process that extends far beyond initial market traction. To achieve longevity and sustainable growth, there are several areas you need to focus on and specific actions you must take. Let's explore these in depth.

Investing in a Culture of Continuous Learning and Innovation

Innovation in SaaS businesses is not merely an advantage; it is a requirement. To stay competitive and relevant, you must cultivate a workplace that encourages curiosity, experimentation, and learning.

Encourage Learning: Offer learning incentives like courses and workshops, subscriptions to online learning platforms like Coursera or Udemy. Regularly invite industry experts for in-house training sessions.

Promote Experimentation: Allow time and resources for employees to work on innovative projects related to your business. Google's '20% time', which encourages developers to spend 20% of their time on side projects, is a famous example.

Recognize and Reward Innovation: Publicly acknowledge and reward innovative ideas and solutions. It not only motivates the innovator but also encourages others to think creatively.

Building and Nurturing Your Team

Your team plays a critical role in the success of your SaaS business. Invest in them not just as employees but as individuals.

Professional Development: Facilitate the ongoing development of your team members. Provide role-specific training, leadership programs, and allow them to attend relevant conferences or networking events.

Create a Supportive Work Environment: Cultivate a workspace that encourages collaboration and mutual support. Use tools like Slack or Microsoft Teams for communication and project management platforms like Asana or Trello to promote transparency and teamwork.

Implement Fair and Motivating Compensation Strategies: Ensure your team feels valued by offering competitive salaries, benefits, and performance-based bonuses or equity options.

Staying Ahead with Industry Trends

SaaS is a rapidly evolving industry. Staying updated with the latest trends will ensure your SaaS business continues to meet market demands.

Regular Market Research: Conduct market research regularly to understand emerging trends and shifts in user behavior. Use tools like Google Trends, SEMRush, or Ahrefs to keep track of popular topics and industry chatter.

Networking: Participate in industry events and forums. Platforms like Meetup, Eventbrite, or even LinkedIn groups can help you connect with peers and stay updated with industry happenings.

Continuous Product Development: Use the insights gathered from market research to drive your product development. Continually improve your product to meet changing customer needs and preferences.

Maintaining Robust Financial Health

The financial stability of your SaaS business is crucial for its sustainability.

- Regular Financial Audits: Conduct regular audits to monitor your business's financial health. Pay attention to your burn rate, operating costs, revenue growth, and profitability.

- Efficient Budgeting: Plan and adhere to budgets. Allocate resources strategically across functions – from product development to sales and marketing.

Financial Contingency Planning: Establish a contingency fund for unexpected expenses or market changes. This could be in the form of reserved cash or an untapped line of credit.

Prioritizing Customer Success

Customer satisfaction directly influences the longevity of your SaaS business. Thus, the emphasis on customer success should go beyond your customer service team.

Proactive Customer Success Team: Invest in a customer success team that proactively helps customers achieve their desired outcomes with your product. Use customer success software like Gainsight or Totango to monitor customer health scores and usage patterns.

Regular Customer Feedback: Regularly solicit customer feedback through surveys, in-app prompts, or personal outreach. Use feedback management platforms like UserVoice or Medallia to collect, analyze, and act on customer feedback.

Implementing Customer Success Across the Company: Foster a customer-centric culture across your company. Encourage every team – from product development to marketing – to consider customer success in their strategies.

Diversifying Your Customer Base and Revenue Streams

Avoid over-reliance on a single customer or market segment. Diversification not only reduces risk but also opens up new growth opportunities.

- Explore New Market Segments: Identify potential customer segments that your product could serve. Customizable product features or add-ons can cater to different needs and attract varied users.

- Expand Geographically: If your product is doing well in one geographic location, consider expanding to new regions. Localizing your software and marketing efforts can help in this regard.

- Introduce New Pricing Tiers or Bundles: Offering different pricing tiers or bundling additional services can attract a wider range of customers and increase your revenue.

Sustainability and long-term success in the SaaS business come from a mix of proactive strategies, constant learning, and quick adaptation to changes. In the final chapter, we'll explore the potential exit strategies for your SaaS business, and how to prepare for them.

Chapter 10: Planning and Preparing for Exit Strategies

The final phase in your SaaS journey can involve an exit strategy. This can range from a strategic acquisition to an initial public offering (IPO). Regardless of the path you choose, planning and preparation are crucial to achieving a successful exit. In this chapter, we'll discuss different exit strategies and specific steps you can take to ensure your SaaS business is ready for a successful transition.

Types of Exit Strategies for SaaS Businesses

Acquisition: This is a common exit strategy for SaaS businesses, where another company purchases your business. Acquisitions typically occur when the buying company wants to acquire your technology, customer base, or team. Acquirers can be larger companies in your industry or related industries, private equity firms, or even competitors.

Merger: A merger involves combining your company with another to create a larger, more powerful entity. This strategy is often chosen when two companies can achieve more together than individually, due to synergies in technology, market, or team.

Initial Public Offering (IPO): An IPO involves selling a portion of your company to the public, thus making your company publicly traded. This strategy is typically chosen by larger, more mature SaaS businesses that have substantial revenue and can meet the requirements of public companies.

Management or Employee Buyout (MBO/EBO): This involves selling your company to your management team or employees. This is often a good choice when the team is well-versed in the business operations and has the capacity to take the company forward.

Preparing Your SaaS Business for a Successful Exit

Regardless of the exit strategy you choose, certain steps can make your business more attractive to potential acquirers or investors, and ensure a smoother transition.

Financial Preparation: Ensure that your financial records are accurate and complete. This will involve having clean audits, detailed financial projections, and a well-organized cap table. Tools like Captable.io can assist in managing your capitalization table.

Legal Due Diligence: Make sure that all legal aspects of your business are in order. This includes having clear ownership of intellectual property, no outstanding legal issues, and well-structured employment agreements. Employ a good lawyer who specializes in SaaS businesses to help you navigate these complexities.

Organizational Readiness: Having a well-structured team with defined roles and responsibilities can make your company more appealing to acquirers. If you're planning an MBO or EBO, ensure that the team is capable and ready to take over the business.

Customer Success and Retention: A strong customer base with high retention rates is attractive to buyers and investors. Ensure your customers are satisfied, and consider long-term contracts or renewals to increase customer stability.

Product Maturity and Market Position: A mature product and a strong market position can significantly increase your company's valuation. This might involve having unique features, a strong brand, or strategic partnerships.

Create an Exit Plan: An exit plan outlines your preferred exit strategy and the steps required to achieve it. This document can guide your actions as you prepare for an exit and serve as a valuable tool in negotiations with potential buyers or investors.

Preparing for an exit strategy involves careful planning and organization. Ensure you understand what potential acquirers or investors value in a SaaS business, and start taking steps to position your business accordingly. Remember, the goal is not just to sell your company, but to ensure its continued success beyond the exit.

Chapter 11: Looking Back and Moving Forward

Every SaaS entrepreneur's journey is unique. The lessons learned, the challenges overcome, and the milestones achieved contribute to the unique story of each SaaS business. As we come to the end of this guide, let's reflect on the journey and discuss the future of the SaaS industry.

Reflection on the Journey

Creating and scaling a successful SaaS business is a roller coaster ride of highs and lows. It requires continuous learning, adaptation, and perseverance. It involves more than just building a product; it's about creating value, building relationships, and making a difference.

Reflecting on your journey can offer valuable insights for future endeavors. Ask yourself:

What were the most valuable lessons you learned? Did you discover something about market research that you hadn't considered before? Or did you learn a harsh lesson about the importance of customer success?

What would you do differently if you could start over? Would you spend more time validating your product idea? Or would you change your approach to fundraising?

What achievements are you most proud of? Did you secure a big customer that gave your SaaS business a significant boost? Or did you successfully navigate a major product pivot?

Your reflections can serve as a roadmap for other SaaS entrepreneurs and add a layer of relatability to your journey.

The Future of SaaS

The SaaS industry continues to evolve rapidly, driven by technological advancements and changing customer needs.

AI and Machine Learning: The incorporation of AI and machine learning into SaaS products will continue to rise, offering more personalized and efficient solutions.

- Vertical SaaS: We'll see more SaaS companies focusing on specific industries (vertical SaaS), offering tailored solutions that cater to the unique needs of those industries.

- Micro SaaS: As large SaaS businesses continue to grow, there will be an increase in Micro SaaS businesses. These are small, niche software solutions that serve specific needs not addressed by the larger players.
- Sustainability: As environmental concerns continue to gain prominence, there will be a rising demand for SaaS solutions that support sustainability, either by optimizing resource usage or by enabling businesses to track and reduce their environmental impact.

The exciting thing about SaaS is its dynamic nature. There's always room for innovative ideas, and the opportunities are endless.

Final Words

Your journey in the SaaS world is a marathon, not a sprint. Celebrate your wins, learn from your losses, but most importantly, keep going. Remember, the ultimate goal isn't just to create a successful SaaS business, but to make a positive impact through your solution.

No matter where you are in your SaaS journey, I hope this guide has provided you with valuable insights and practical tips to help you navigate the path ahead. Remember, every challenge is an opportunity, and every setback is a chance to learn and grow.

I, Esad Kılıç, along with my SaaS journey, am a testament to the fact that with the right approach, tenacity, and hard work, you can turn your SaaS dream into a reality. Don't be afraid of the challenges that lie ahead. Embrace them, and you'll come out stronger on the other side.

Good luck, and here's to your SaaS success!

The SaaS Glossary

SaaS (Software as a Service): A software delivery model where applications are hosted and provided to users over the internet, eliminating the need for on-premises installation and maintenance.

MVP (Minimum Viable Product): The most basic version of a product with enough features to satisfy early customers and collect feedback for further development.

API (Application Programming Interface): A set of rules and protocols that allows different software applications to communicate and interact with each other.

CRM (Customer Relationship Management): A system for managing and analyzing customer interactions and data to improve relationships, sales, and customer service.

Churn Rate: The rate at which customers cancel or stop using a SaaS product or service over a specific period, indicating customer attrition.

CAC (Customer Acquisition Cost): The average cost a company incurs to acquire a new customer, including marketing, sales, and onboarding expenses.

LTV (Customer Lifetime Value): The predicted net profit generated from a customer over their entire relationship with a company, providing insight into customer value and retention strategies.

ARPU (Average Revenue Per User): The average monthly or annual revenue generated by each user of a SaaS product, indicating the profitability of each customer.

MRR (Monthly Recurring Revenue): The predictable and regular revenue generated from subscription fees or recurring charges on a monthly basis.

SLA (Service Level Agreement): A contract between a SaaS provider and a customer that defines the expected service quality, uptime, and support levels.

Scalability: The ability of a SaaS application or infrastructure to handle increased user demand and growth without sacrificing performance or stability.

UI (User Interface): The graphical or visual interface through which users interact with a SaaS application, including screens, menus, buttons, and other elements.

UX (User Experience): The overall experience and satisfaction users have while interacting with a SaaS product, focusing on usability, accessibility, and enjoyment.

IaaS (Infrastructure as a Service): A cloud computing model that provides virtualized computing resources, such as virtual machines, storage, and networks, to users over the internet.

PaaS (Platform as a Service): A cloud computing model that provides a platform for developers to build, deploy, and manage applications without the need for infrastructure management.

Hybrid Cloud: A cloud computing environment that combines both public and private cloud infrastructure, allowing organizations to utilize the benefits of both models.

Microservices: An architectural approach where software applications are built as a collection of small, independent services that can be developed, deployed, and scaled separately.

Devops: A set of practices that combines software development (Dev) and IT operations (Ops) to improve collaboration, automation, and efficiency in the software delivery process.

Agile Methodology: An iterative and incremental approach to software development, focusing on flexibility, collaboration, and delivering working software in short development cycles.

Data Security: Measures and protocols implemented to protect sensitive data and ensure confidentiality, integrity, and availability of information within a SaaS application.

Big Data: Extremely large and complex data sets that require specialized tools and techniques to store, process, and analyze, providing valuable insights for decision-making.

Machine Learning: An application of artificial intelligence (AI) that enables software systems to learn and improve from data without explicit programming, allowing them to make predictions or take actions.

IoT (Internet of Things): A network of interconnected physical devices embedded with sensors, software, and connectivity to exchange data and perform tasks without human intervention.

Compliance: Adherence to legal, industry-specific, or regulatory standards and requirements applicable to a SaaS business, such as GDPR, HIPAA, or PCI DSS.

Data Analytics: The process of examining large datasets to uncover patterns, trends, and insights that can inform decision-making and optimize business operations.

Customer Success: A proactive approach to ensuring customer satisfaction, adoption, and long-term success by providing support, guidance, and value-added services.

Fundraising Rounds: Stages of investment funding in a SaaS startup, typically starting with a Seed round and progressing to Series A, B, C, and beyond.

Exit Strategy: A plan outlining how a SaaS company will monetize or divest its business, including options like acquisition, merger, IPO, or management/employee buyout.

Bootstrapping: Building and growing a SaaS business without external investment or venture capital funding, relying on revenue generation and organic growth.

Ecosystem: The network of interconnected software applications, services, and integrations that surround and complement a SaaS product, creating a comprehensive solution for customers.

www.ingramcontent.com/pod-product-compliance
Lightning Source LLC
Chambersburg PA
CBHW072235230526
45466CB00024B/1984